Diary of a Journey through Upper Canada

John Goldie, Wm. Tyrreli and Co.

DIARY OF A JOURNEY

THROUGH UPPER CANADA

AND SOME OF THE

NEW ENGLAND STATES,

1819

BY

JOHN GOLDIE.

TORONTO:
WM. TYRRELL & CO.
1897.

Introduction.

***

I T is to be regretted that the strictly botanical journal which Mr. Goldie kept during the journey described in this diary was lost by fire. The present journal contains observations both upon the general aspect of the country through which he passed, and some few notes on the flora.

The following is a brief sketch of the life of Mr. Goldie, the author of this diary.

Mr. John Goldie was born near the village of Kirkoswold, Ayrshire, Scotland, on March 21st, 1793.

In early life, after receiving a thorough training in the Science of Botany, and in practical gardening, he became connected with the Botanic Gardens at Glasgow. Among his fellow students was Mr. Douglass, after whom the " Douglass Pine " was named, and who travelled extensively in British Columbia and Oregon, and was afterwards killed in the Sandwich Islands.

Mr. Goldie was married in 1815, to Margaret Dunlop Smith, daughter of James Smith of Monkwood Grove, Ayrshire, a prominent Botanist and Nurseryman. Shortly after his marriage, the English Government having determined to send an expedition to the coast of Africa to explore the Congo River, Mr. Goldie, after passing a strict examination, was selected to accompany the expedition as Botanist. At the last moment he was superceded, to which circumstance he perhaps owed his life, as the person selected (by political favour) to take his place as well as a great many of the officers and crew died of the coast fever, and the expedition was abandoned.

In June, 1817, at the instance of Mr. Wm. Hooker, afterwards Sir. Wm., Mr. Goldie sailed from Leith for America. He landed at Halifax, and remained for some time botanizing in that neighborhood. From there he went to Quebec, carrying with him all the roots and specimens he had so far obtained ; these, together with the produce of two weeks research in the neighborhood of Quebec, he put on board a vessel bound for Greenock, but never heard of them afterwards. From Quebec he proceed to Montreal, where he met Mr. Pursh, author of the North American Flora. From Montreal he travelled on foot to Albany, (N.Y.), and then proceeded by water to New York. Here he stayed but a short time ; these months he now employed in exploring the Eastern part of New Jersey, which he considered a rich field for the botanist. This summers' specimens he now shipped at New York for Scotland, and again was doomed to disappointment, as he never afterwards obtained any intelligence of them.

During the winter of 1818, he taught school at a small place near the Mohawk River. In April he proceeded to Montreal, where he expected to find Mr. Pursh, through whose influence he had hoped to be able to go with the traders to the North-West country. But Mr. Pursh had left, so this summer to make ends meet he was obliged to fall back on the spade. Two days in each week he devoted to botanizing. In the autumn he shipped his collection of plants, and for the third time misfortune overtook him, for the vessel in which they were was totally wrecked in the St. Lawrence. The following winter he did not do very much, but by the beginning of June, 1819, he had saved a small amount of money, and having borrowed some more from a friend, he commenced his journey which is recorded in this Diary. As a result of this two years' work in America, he introduced into Europe many new and rare plants, a list of which is to be found in the *Edinburgh Philosophical Journal*, (April, 1822-vol. vi.) Amongst these was the fern *Aspidium Goldianum*, which was so named by his friend Hooker. Mr. Goldie's original description of this fern will be found at the end of this diary.

About this time, the Emperor of Russia established a Botanical Garden at St. Petersburg, and Mr. Goldie was employed to make a collection of plants for it. The curator of of the Gardens at St. Petersburg being an old college friend, he was enabled through him to introduce many rare plants into England. During his residence in Russia, Mr. Goldie made extensive botanical explorations. About the year 1830, he visited Russia for a second time, and travelled in Siberia following his favorite pursuit.

Having formed a favorable opinion of Canada as a place of residence, on his visits in 1817—1819, he brought his family here in 1844, and settled near the village of Ayr, Ont., where he continued to reside until his death in July, 1886. Mr. Goldie was thus in his 94th year when he died. During his lifetime he corresponded with many prominent botanists, and after he came to Canada, more particularly with his friend Sir Wm. Hooker.

DIARY FOR THE YEAR 1819.

On June 4th, 1819, I commenced my long talked of journey to examine the natural but more particularly the botanical productions of Upper Canada and of the States, in the vicinity of of the Lakes. In the course of my journey I shall give the highest at which I happen to observe the thermometer. To-day it thundered toward the South ; thermometer 76. This night I stopped at St. Anne's, at the upper end of the Island of Montreal, and in the forenoon of the 5th, reached the Grand River which is five or six hundred yards wide at this place, and proceeding along the bank of the St. Lawrence, came to a small village called Coteau de Lac. There is a fort here which was occupied during the late American War, and which at present contains a few soldiers. Weather fair ; thermometer 86.

6th. I left the road which goes alongside the river and took the more inland one which passes through Glengarry. The land along this road is pretty thickly settled, and all by French people until you come within four or five miles of the Upper Province, in which place is a continued swampy wood. In the afternoon I got through the woods and the Lower Province and entered the County of Glengarry, of which the Highlanders boast so much. It appears rather singular how much the land differs on the boundries of the two provinces. From the Coteau de Lac all along the small River de L'Isle the country is generally level, and free from stones, but, as soon as you cross a small rivulet, which on this side is the boundary of Glengarry, the whole ground is covered with stones and is considerably uneven. To-day the weather was very hot. In the evening, thunder to the West. Thermometer 92, at sunset 78. Mosquitoes in myriads.

7th. I passed through the West of Glengarry and came into Cornwall which has the same appearance as Glengarry as to the land, but there is a considerable difference in the people. The inhabitants of Glengarry retain all the habits, customs, etc., of the Highlanders of Scotland.

8th. I travelled all day along the St. Lawrence which has a fine appearance, and is thickly interspersed with islands. The soil along the river is sandy, but seems, when properly managed to produce good crops. Grain of all sorts is a great deal more advanced here than in any other place I have passed through. This day I passed that bloody spot, which will long be known in the annals of history, Chrystler's Farm, where a handful of the British, overcame a large army of the Americans and prevented them from making an attack upon Montreal.

9th. I arrived early in the afternoon at Prescott, which is a small village, but contains some respectable buildings. A little before one enters the village there is a small battery, formed by enclosing a considerable extent of grove with the adjacent earth collected into a ridge. In the inside there are contained barracks for the soldiers, etc. Opposite Prescott on the south side of the St. Lawrence, lies the town of Ogdensburg which is a handsome looking village and of considerable extent. After leaving Prescott, I travelled alongside the river as far as Brockville, twelve miles from Prescott, where I remained for the night. I was informed that within a very few years past Brockville consisted of only two or three houses, but now there are at least a dozen houses, which, either in quality or elegance may compare with any in Upper Canada, besides a great many others of inferior quality. This morning was pleasant, but towards mid-day the wind rose rather high, and from the dusty state of the roads travelling became rather disagreeable. Weather, morning clear, cloudy in the afternoon ; thermometer 77.

10th. I remained at Brockville examining the vegetable productions in the vicinity. To-day when in the woods, a little distance from the town, I saw the spot where the remains of a man were found this spring, after the snow went off. He was supposed to have been murdered in the fall. The place where he was found was within thirty or fourty yards of a public road. He was laid behind an old tree which had fallen, and considerable pains had been taken to cover him over with branches, leaves, etc. Part of his clothes still remain in the snow where he was lying. Weather fair; thermometer 69.

11th. In the morning I set out on my journey for Kingston. The road follows the river for a few miles, and then goes more inland, so that you do not see the St. Lawrence until you arrive at Gananoque thirty-three miles from Brockville. The face of the country now assumes a more uneven and barren aspect. Six miles from Brockville you cross a creek with very steep banks, and whose course appears as if it had been cut out of the solid rock. For a long way afterwards a house is to be seen only in three or four miles, the land being so rocky that it is incapable of cultivation. Even in many places where settled I should think that it is scarcely worth the labor that has been bestowed upon it. As I approached Gananoque I found the country very wild, and not a house in four or five miles. The forepart of this day was very pleasant, but towards evening it threatened rain, however it kept off with the exception of a small shower, until after sunset, when just as I came to the door of the inn where I slept, it rained for some time remarkably heavy, quite in the American style. Thermometer 80.

12th. I left the village of Gananoque which contains only a few buildings, and again entered the woods out of which I did not get until my arrival at Kingston, a distance of twenty four miles, the country all the way being nothing but rock, and very thinly settled. Last night and to-day I have been exceedingly tormented by mosquitoes and another small black fly which is still worse. Wherever they pierce the skin the blood flows very copiously, so that my face and neck were all besmeared with blood, and afterwards had the appearance of a person infected with the smallpox. Weather to-day pleasant, fair ; thermometer 82.

13th. I remained in Kingston. To-day very pleasant, fair ; thermometer 70 ; frost at night.

14th. Having arranged my affairs, I left Kingston about ten o'clock and proceeded by the front road for York, (now Toronto). This road is at some distance from the Lake for about seven miles, and afterwards lies close alongside the Lake. The shore of Ontario is in most places low and quite rocky. In a few places it is of considerable height and perpendicular. As far as the Bay of Quinte, one scarcely sees any appearance of a lake of any extent, but only a pretty large river, on account of its being so filled with islands. Some of the islands are large, and have a few settlers on them ; others are completely covered with wood, and in a state of nature. I consider it a very pleasant situation all along the Lake, and it is thickly settled, but still the land is very rocky, although now and then you may see a small spot which appears to be very good. To-day I have met with a number of interesting plants, some of which are new to me. I lodged at night in Earnest Town, a small village with a few respectable buildings, and an old unshapely church. It is twenty five miles from Kingston. Weather very pleasant, and was fair ; thermometer in the afternoon 84.

15th. Having travelled about seven miles I was stopped a little while by rain but it soon cleared up and I crossed over to the Bay of Quinte and went along the south side of it, until I came to Mr. Fisher's where I remained for some time. Thermometer 72. I did not leave this until the twenty-first.

16th. Fair ; thermometer. 84.

17th. Thunder to the North in the afternoon which continued most of the night with very vivid lightning. Thermometer 84.

18th. Morning fair, thunder to the West through the day; thermometer 90.

19th. I intended to have set out but the wind was so high that I could not get across the Bay. Fair; thermometer 78.

20th. Being Sunday I remained here as I was in good quarters. Fair; thermometer 78.

21st. After breakfast I commenced my journey for York, (Toronto). After going about five miles alongside the Bay I crossed it, and went for a number of miles through a pretty thickly settled country. In the afternoon I came again upon the South side of the Bay of Quinte which lies in a circular form, so that the head of it comes almost in contact with the Lake. I got now completely into the bush. The first house that I came to was seven or eight miles distant from the last. Although the sun was yet high, I thought it advisable to stop here for the night, being informed that the next house was six miles distant. I am told that it is the most public of any from Kingston to York. To-day I have met with a number of plants which I have not before seen, some of them very interesting. Crops appear good, but there is a great want of rain in this part of the country. Day fair; thermometer 84. This night I heard for the first time the well known Whip-Poor-Will.

22nd. The house where I lodged last night being closely surrounded with woods, and full of chinks and crevices, admitted the mosquitoes so plentifully that I could scarcely get any sleep, which circumstance caused me to stir betimes this morning. The weather was fair, but a little cold. At an hour after sunrise the thermometer was 51. I did not see many houses this morning until I travelled ten miles when I came again to the Bay of Quinte, along which I walked, until at last I reached its head which was eight miles further. Where the Bay terminates it is only about a mile distant from the Lake. A canal could very easily unite the two, if there was as much trade as would pay interest for expenses of cutting it. The land along the Bay appears to have been settled for a considerable time. In some places the soil is good, in others it is very indifferent. There are a few good looking orchards here, and some lately planted, but as none of the trees are grafted or budded they are of considerably less value. Leaving the Carrying Place, which is the name of this Isthmus, the road goes at some distance from the the Lake through woods but thinly settled, and, which in many places exhibit marks of being but very lately under cultivation. From the Carrying Place till where I stopped for the night, I observed nothing remarkable, except that I met with more streams of pure water in the evening than I remember to have seen in all the places I have visited in America. I was so pleased to find good water that it was with some reluctance that I passed any of them without drinking. The day was good, although some showers went about to the South and West ; thermometer 80.

23rd. I started pretty early and after travelling until about mid-day I passed a town called Hamilton, situated close to Lake. It contains but a few houses, some of which are very good. Before I had gone two miles further, a thunderstorm arose which continued for a considerable time, and obliged me to stop. There had been no rain here for a considerable time before, and the roads were become remarkably dry and dusty ; which with the great heat came to be very severe upon the feet, so that, although the rain made the road a little muddy, it was more pleasant travelling. At some distance afterwards I crossed Smith's Creek, where there are a few buildings. After leaving the creek you get into a sandy barren wood, without any house for same miles. I only travelled six miles further, by which time the sun was setting. The country through which I passed to-day was much the same as seen yesterday, some good and some very indifferent. Rye seems to be the grain that grows best here. There appears to be very little attention paid to the cultivation of potatoes in this part of the country. In the course of a day's travel one will not see an acre of them. The people in this locality have been for some days past busy in hoeing their corn. This day was fair except the shower mentioned before, and another a little afterwards which passed to the South; thermometer 72.

24th. I arose with the sun, and, after going two miles, I got into what are called the nine-mile woods. A short time ago there was not a house all this distance, but lately there have been three or four log ones built. The cause of there being so few settlers here is not, as in many instances, the barrenness of the soil, which in these woods is very good, but the proprietors of this place have got hold of nearly all the land and will neither clear it themselves, nor sell it to those who would do so. As a law has been passed obliging every person to keep the road in repair opposite his property, it is probable that this will induce them to make some better use of this and many other pieces of land, than they have hitherto done. The morning being calm the mosquitoes were extremely numerous and almost insufferable. After leaving the wood there are a few miles cleared along the road, after which you came into the five-mile woods, which are still un-settled. These places are likely to retain their original appella-tions however inappropriate they may be in a short period. I travelled only a few miles further to-night, and lodged exactly thirty miles from York. The land appears better here than lower down, and if properly cultivated and manured would produce luxuriant crops. For three days past I have seen nothing interesting to the botanist, which circumstances is not calculated to elevate the spirits and make one forget the fatigue of travell-ing. This day was fair; thermometer 80.

25th. As I did not intend to go into York, I travelled to-day but slowly, sometimes in woods, and sometimes in cleared land. Before mid-day I passed a creek which lay very low, so that the road is very steep on each side. All the declivity on the east side was completely covered with the "*Penstemon pubescens*" such a quantity of which I never expected to see in one place. For a number of miles to-day I passed through barren sandy pine woods which it is probable will never be cleared. In the morning I met a number of Indians and squaws. One of the men was very drunk. He told me that he was crazy with taking too much bitters this morning. One of them had no clothing upon him except a piece of cloth about a foot in length and breadth which hung before him. I stopped for the night six miles from York, there being no other inn upon this road nearer to it. As I was only a short distance from the Lake, I went to it, but found the shore at least two hundred feet high and very abrupt, in some places almost perpendicular, so that it was with considerable difficulty that I could approach the water. The bank is almost entirely composed of sand, which approaches to clay after a considerable depth. I expected to have found a number of plants here, but was disappointed. Having bathed in the Lake I returned to my lodging. This day was very pleasant, there being a considerable breeze, which both kept one cool and kept off these tormentors the mosquitoes. Thermometer 76.

26th. I went on for York. As soon as I left the tavern where I lodged, I entered into what in this part of the country the people call a Pine Plain, but what in some of the States would be denominated a Pine Barren, which is a very appropriate name for such kind of land. I found the vegetable productions here in many places similar to what they are in New Jersey. The woods continue until you come within less than thee miles of York, where the land is generally cleared, although it does not appear to be anything superior in quality. I came into York about ten o'clock and intended to have remained at least one day in it, but I was not long here until I changed my mind, and left it for Lake Simcoe. When at Kingston I left the greater part of my specimen paper together with all my other articles which I did not immediately need, to be sent to York by the

Steamboat which only sails between these two places three times a month. It happened that they had been put on board a schooner addressed to the care of a storekeeper, but he not observing any mention of them in the Bill of Lading which he received with some articles of his own, made no inquiry about them, and they were not delivered. When I called at the store and could find no account of my things, I did not feel easy, as I had my book that I carried along with me quite full of specimens, and my hat was as full of insects, so that I could do nothing more until I had the present cargo disposed of. Of the appearance of York I shall say nothing until a future period. I started in the afternoon and travelled eight miles due North on the road to Simcoe. This day was very hot, fair; thermometer 86. I forgot to mention above, that, just as I was inquiring for my knapsack the schooner which brought it from Kingston returned from Niagara, so I went on board and found it. If I had not luckily been there just at this time it would have been carried back to Kingston, which would have been an unfortunate circumstance for me.

27th. It was about six in the morning when I started, and in a short time it was so hot that travelling became very oppressive. At nine a.m. the thermometer stood 84. The roads were now again become remarkably dry and dusty, so that when any wheeled carriage passed I was involved in a cloud of dust which was extremely disagreeable. This is the best road that I have seen in Upper Canada, and since I left York there have been more waggons travelling this road than on all those that I have seen since I left Montreal. Having gone on slowly I arrived in the evening at what is called the Upper Landing Place, which is about nine miles by water from Lake Simcoe. I stopped at the farthest house upon this road and have bespoken a week's lodging here, as I expect that it is a spot very interesting for the botanist. Day fair; thermometer 91.

28th.   Day fair and extremely hot.   At nine a.m. the thermometer stood 90.   About mid-day there was a thunderstorm which however mostly passed to the Southward ; thermometer 93.

29th.   Rain in the morning : in the afternoon it cleared up, but towards evening became again cloudy ; thermometer 77.   As the house at which I stop is situated in the midst of woods and marshes, the mosquitoes have been exceedingly troublesome these two days past.   It is almost impossible to sleep during the night, for they are quite as plentiful and every way as michievous as during the day,

30th.   Rained very heavy all day ; thermometer 70.

July. 1st   Rained for the greater part of the day ; thermometer 64.

2nd.   Rained during the forenoon, cloudy in the afternoon ; thermometer 64.

3rd.   Cloudy in the morning, but cleared up in the afternoon. This evening a company of the 70th Regiment from Drummond Island in Lake Huron, arrived here.   They have been up the country for two years, and have been exchanged for two companies of the 68th.   Thermometer 78.

4th.   Was fair and pleasant.   This evening I saw a comet to the north-west, about an hour after sunset.   Its tail could be seen very distinctly and was of considerable length.   Some superstitious people here are firm in the belief that it prognosticates an immediate war with the United States, as one appeared before the late war.   All around this part of the county you hear of wars and rumours of war.   For what purpose some people invent and publish such stories, I cannot imagine, except it be to make their neighbours believe that they are possessed of more foresight and a greater share of sagacity than others.   All such reports appear to be totally destitute of any foundation.   Thermometer 73. This being the last day of my abode here, I shall mention a few things more concerning this part of the country.   Lake Sincoe is between thirty and forty miles long and of considerable breadth, but I could not ascertain accurately how many miles. On the South side there is what is called a river, which although of no great breadth, has yet sufficient depth to allow schooners to come to the Upper Landing Place which is nine miles from the Lake and thirty-six from York. This river apparently is stagnant and the water has more the appearance of flowing from the Lake than into it. After crossing the Lake there is nine miles of a portage and then there is water carriage all the way to Lake Huron. It is very probable that at no very distant period this will become the most frequented of all the routes to the north-west. At the present time there are no houses nor stores on the north side of Simcoe at the portage, which make it very inconvenient and render the goods transported liable to be injured by the weather. Since a Steamboat has commenced to sail on Lake Erie the cheapest and most expeditious mode of sending down the furs from the interior is by that route, although it is four hundred miles longer than by Simcoe. There is only one schooner upon the Lake, which is sufficient for all the trade at present. Since I came here I have seen a number of rare plants, and some of them are non-descripts. There is a species of *Asclepias* with orange flowers very handsome, a species of *Euphorbium* with white flowers, a *Ranunculus*, together with some other plants not in flower that I had never before seen. If a person could spend a season here he might expect to find many plants not yet described.

5th. This morning was remarkably cold for this season of the year. I could not get away before ten a.m. As the day was good I took it easy and stopped twelve miles from York. Having travelled this road before I need say nothing concerning it now. Fair; thermometer 80.

6th. On the morning of the 6th I came into York, where I remained all this day. York is situated upon a Bay formed by a narrow piece of land which stretches out from the eastern side of the town, and almost incloses a small portion of the Lake, the outlet being to the south-west. The harbour is not at all adapted for shipping. The bullrushes grow some feet above water at nearly one hundred yards distance from the land. There are two piers of wood which project a great way into the water, where the Steamboat and the Schooners load and unload. Upon the neck of land nearly south of the City is a lighthouse which is the only building there except a log house at its extremity. York is very inferior in extent to Kingston, and also in my opinion in its situation. It can only be said, strictly speaking, to possess one street, for the cross ones scarcely yet deserve that name. Most of the buildings are very good, but are all with the exception of two or three of wood. There is only one Church in the City, which is Episcopalian. As yet they have not a Presbyterian Church, but when Presbyterians have service it must be in some building appropriated to some other purpose. The street is without pavement. When I was here I saw them mending it, which was accomplished by first turning it completely up with a plough as if to sow grain and afterwards throwing the earth from the sides and heights upon the middle and into the hollows. Although such streets would not do in Britain, yet here they are even better than if they were paved. The ground is very dry and sandy. The summer is generally dry and the number of carriages that travel the streets is comparatively few. When Winter commences it is of no importance of what material streets are made. In that season frost and snow make all roads alike. York is without any fortification, and the public buildings were burned by the Americans in the late war. About three miles above the town are the barracks for the soldiers, and the Governor's House. I saw the 70th regiment go on board the Steamboat *Frontenac* for Kingston. This is the only Steamboat that sails between York and Kingston. She makes only three trips a month, leaving Kingston upon the first, eleventh and twenty-first of each month. After touching at York she sails to Niagara and returns by the same route. This boat is a great deal larger than any other that I have ever seen. There are also a few Schooners that trade between this and Kingston, Niagara and the American side of the Lake. From York I could have sailed to Niagara in a few hours and for a small sum, but I preferred travelling by land, although the distance is ninety miles, while by water it is only thirty. I was informed that the fog which arises over the Falls can be observed here on a clear and calm morning.

7th. In the morning there was a shower which detained me from setting out as early as I had intended. There being a Schooner here which was to sail to Niagara this afternoon, I considered it better to send all my spare articles by her, which would cost me only one shilling and three pence (1/3), than to have a load to carry for one hundred miles. Within two miles of York, to the West, there are a few very elegant buildings, superior to most in Canada. Three miles from York you come into a sandy pine barren which continues for five miles and in which there are one or two houses. I had not been long here when I met with ample compensation for the fatigue of travelling by land. This was as good a botanical spot as any that I ever was in. I wish that there were more of the pine barrens even than what there are. Having so much employ-ment this day I was unable to proceed far on my journey. I believe I stopped fifteen miles from York. This day was calm and very sultry, with occasional heavy clouds ; thermometer 90.

8th. I never passed a more disagreeable night in America than the last one. Being sleepy I went to bed early, but I was not long there, when I would have been extremely glad to have been able to fall asleep. The mosquitoes were the chief cause of disturbance, although not altogether the only one. Whenever I have it in my power now to choose, I shall take particular care to inspect the state of the tavern windows, so that whatever may be inside I may be free from external intruders. The country through which I passed to-day was generally well settled and of rather good quality, but all inclining to sand. This day I crossed three considerable creeks which run very much below the level of the adjacent land ; their banks are both high and very steep, so that it must have been with a good deal of difficulty that a road has been made across them. The road is mostly composed of wood which forms a barrier to the earth that is cut from the bank. After travelling about twenty-eight miles I came alongside the West corner of Lake Ontario, where the first object that I noticed was what appeared to me to be a great body of smoke on the opposite side of the Lake ; but you may guess my incredulous surprise and pleased astonishment when I was informed that that was the spray of the Great Falls. It appeared very distinctly and as if at no great distance ; and in the calm mornings and evenings the sound of the Falls is distinctly heard at this place which is thirty miles distant in a direct line. As you proceed along the west end of Ontario you pass between it and what is properly called Burlington Bay, but its common appell-ation here is the Little Lake. It is seven miles across in the widest place and lies close alongside the other Lake for five miles. The road passes along the beach which lies between the Lakes, and is from one hundred to two hundred yards wide. The only connection between the Lake and the Bay is about sixty yards wide, and through this the current was setting into the Bay, when I passed here. I went two miles from the Lake by which time the sun had sunk below the Western forests, and I thought it best to halt for the night. Where I remained is called Stoney Creek, and has three taverns within one hundred yards. I was careful to survey them before entering and pitched upon one which was dignified by the title of hotel. This day was fair with occasional clouds ; thermometer 90.

9th. This day take it all in all I consider the hottest that I have ever felt. The morning was very calm. The road lay in a low situation with high land on one side and woods on both. From seven a.m. until sunset the mercury stood above 80, with very little wind all day. I travelled this day twenty-eight miles and came to the twelve-mile creek, being that distance from Niagara. The road all along this way is very good, and the land I consider as good as any I have seen since I left Montreal. In all the low lands from Stoney Creek, where I remained last night, I have observed numbers of the *Plantanus Occidentalis* being the first that I have seen in their natural state. One of the greatest hardships which I endured here and in many other places, was the want of good water. There is not a drop to be got except where the inhabitants have dug wells, which only comparatively few have done, rather subjecting themselves to one of the greatest inconveniences in life than be at the trouble of digging for a few feet, when they might possess abundance of excellent water. People here are beginning to cut their hay and secure it. I see that here they have found no better method of building it in ricks than in most parts of America, building the hay round a long pole previously fastened in the ground. The top of the pole remains some feet above the hay all winter, and, as there is no thatch used, I do not think that a more effectual method could be adopted to rot the hay completely. The corn seems to grow remarkably well here ; it is far superior to what is found lower down. the Lake. Day fair ; thermometer 94.

10th. I only went as far as Niagara this day. This town is situated at the junction of the River St. Lawrence with Lake Ontario, in an agreeable situation. This town was formerly called Newark, and was burnt by the Americans during the late war, not one house being spared, so that all the present town has been built since that period. It contains a number of streets, but none of them are yet filled up with houses ; however, I thnk it as at least half as large as York. On the north side of the town and close to the Lake is a Fort named Mississago, and on the south side, on the bank of the St. Lawrence is Fort George. There are also barracks in the vicinity of the Town. At present there are about three hundred

of the 68th Regiment stationed here.   The only building worthy
of particular notice is the Jail, which stands about a quarter of a
mile out of the town.   It is a large two-storey house of brick,
very handsome, and is considered to be the finest building in
Canada.   At present it holds within its walls the celebrated
Gourley.   A few of the Niagara newspapers that I have seen
are nearly filled with his writings and those of his opponents.
However, I believe that he generally remains last on the field,
which is commonly considered a proof of victory.   One of his
papers which was of great length, I read, and, from the senti-
ments it contains, I cannot think that he is so dangerous a
character as the men in power would have people believe.   He
is very free in giving his opinion concerning the character of the
Governors, and I suspect his greatest fault is speaking too many
truths, which are not thought to be seasonable or agreeable.   He
asserts positively that the Duke of Richmond came to Canada
solely for the purpose of making money, and that Sir P. Maitland
made a runaway marriage with a daughter of the Duke's
in France, but that peace was made through the mediation
of the Duke of Wellington under whom Sir Peregrine was serving
at that time ; and that this connection elevated him greatly and
eventually made him Governor of Upper Canada.   I was informed that the width of the river here is three quarters of a
mile.   On the opposite side, on a point of land that projects a
little way into the Lake stands Fort Niagara, belonging to the
Americans.   If sufficiently manned it is said to be strong.
During the late war the British took it by surprise, but it was
given up at the conclusion of peace.   This day was very hot in
the forenoon ; it was fair, but in the afternoon there were showers
to the South and lightning in the evening ; thermometer 94.

11th.   On the 11th, after breakfast I departed on my way
to the Falls, which are distant from the town of Niagara
fourteen miles.   All the way to Queenstown the road is close to
the river.   The banks of the St. Lawrence here are very high and

steep, but not rocky. This is as pleasant a walk as any that I have had in America. I cannot say that the land is good ; it is sand, but yet the crops look well, and every house here has an orchard. Cherries are very abundant in this part of the country, and there are also quite a number of peaches. To-day I have seen, and eaten a greater number of cherries than I think I have ever done before. The cherry trees are all planted close alongside the road, and any person that passes may help himself from them. Having come to Queenstown which is quite a small village, I was anxious to get upon the field of battle, by which its name has attained celebrity. Close to the upper end of the town, the spot was pointed out to me where the brave General Brock was killed. It is quite near the road, and is marked by a number of thorn bushes which form a rude circle. They were not however planted on that account, but grew here long before that time From Niagara to Queenstown the land is quite level, but at the south end of the latter it rises very suddenly in the form of a ridge at right angles to the river. This ridge is called Queenstown Heights, and on it the battle was fought that is called by the same name. A similar ridge is seen on the opposite side of the river, and it looks as if at some period the two had been continuous. The bed of the river is very much contracted when opposite the Heights, and the banks are steep and rise to a great height above the water. A number of Americans were driven over these heights into the river, when attempting to seek safety in flight. When I reached the top of the Heights I sat down for some time to enjoy the prospect before me, on the very spot where many a man had lost his life. I was here at noon when the mercury stood 84. With mingled sensations of pleasure and melancholy I viewed this and some other similar scenes where many hundreds of my fellow-creatures had been hurled into eternity. As the ground rises here so suddenly, I expected that on reaching the top of the Heights I would have an extensive view on the opposite side at least as far as the Falls, but I was astonished to find that instead of there being a declivity it was all level to the South and West. There is no perceptible rise in the land all the way to Lake Erie, I am informed, so that it seems as if the Falls had been originally a that place. The banks of the river now become rocky and fromt one to two hundred feet in height. After travelling three miles above this, I was informed that there was a whirlpool in the river (which was now distant from the road one and one half miles), well worth the attention of a stranger. Having abundance of time I determined to take a view of the whirlpool, which some people told me was as great a curiosity as the Falls. I found this whirlpool to be caused by a very sudden bend in of the river. Immediately above this the river is very much contracted, which causes it to flow with great rapidity; so that when its former direction is changed at a very acute angle, instead of rounding the projection of the rock, the water runs past the course that it afterwards assumes, and forms a capacious basin, round which it is whirled.

The sight cannot be called sublime, yet it is well worth attention. The water is almost smooth on the surface, but by its whirling and contortions in every direction, with the foam on the top, shows that it is greatly agitated below the surface. There is a something of grandeur and dignity in its stillness which much pleased me even more than if it had been in a greater commotion. The banks here are very high; near the top they are perpendicular, but nearer the water they have a slope, this part of them being covered with trees. The river here is certainly narrow and must be remarkably deep, although from the top of the bank I found myself very much deceived by the distance. I believe that there are few people but would think at first sight that they could cast a stone to the opposite side of the river. I almost thought I could, but upon trying I was not able to throw one into the edge of the water, although it appeared to be almost quite under where I stood. A ladder of twenty-eight steps is built down the face of the rock, by which you can approach the water's edge. On the rocks here I found two species of little ferns which I had not hitherto come across. Returning again to the road I set out for the Falls which were now distant only four miles. By this time I was much disappointed in not hearing their sound, having thought that before this I would have heard them roaring like the loudest thunder. When I got within two miles of them, I could hear them distinctly enough, but far from being loud. The afternoon being well spent I did not think of visiting them to-night, but remained at a tavern one mile distant from these celebrated wonders of nature. This day was hot and fair ; thermometer 90.

12th. This morning it rained a little, so that I did not go out until after breakfast to visit the Falls. On approaching them I found the ground in their vicinity to exhibit a very different appearance from what I had expected. Instead of high rocks and precipices above the Falls, and valleys and glens below them, all is perfectly level in appearance. Indeed you have rather to descend as you approach them. At the distance of two hundred yards there is nothing to be seen in the banks of the river that would lead you to expect any such thing as Falls at this place. Before getting to Table Rock, one must descend a pretty steep bank, and being down you immediately find yourself on Table Rock at the very edge of the falling water. These water-falls have been generally considered one of the grandest and most sublime sights in nature. I shall not dispute it. They certainly are grand, but do not exceed or even equal the conception of them that I had formed. For me they possess none of that awful and terrific sublimity which I have beheld in a stormy and tempestuous ocean. I was extremely disappointed with respect to the sound of the falling of so great a body of water. After remaining some time above I went down below to the bottom of the falls, having read that the sound there was far greater than above, but still had the mortification of being disappointed. Two people might stand at the edge of the falls and each hear the other when speaking in an ordinary tone as well as if they were a mile distant from them. There is no perceptible descent in the ground all the way from Lake Erie to Queenstown, so that the height of the falls is caused by the greater depth of the bed of the river below than above them. The river above the falls is very broad and runs from about south-east to north-west, but immediately below them it takes a sudden bend to the north-east. Above the descent the river is nearly as high as the adjacent country while below, all the way to Queenstown, it is as much beneath the bank as the height of the falls. The river is divided into two parts by Goat Island, as is generall well-known, and the greater portion of the water runs on the Canadian side. Goat Island is the largest, being, I imagine, half-a-mile in length, but there are ten more islands immediately adjoining it, eight on the American side and two on the Canadian, which are not commonly mentioned at all, at least I have seen no account of them. For nearly a mile above the falls the bed of the river descends a number of feet, being very uneven with great breaks in the rocks which form the bottom of the river and which cause the water to be extremely rough and to have a very rapid current. The Fall on the north side is nearly in the form of a semicircle ; the middle, from the greater quantity of water falling, wearing much faster than the sides. From its shape it is called the Horse-shoe Fall. The Fall on the other side is indented in many places but not nearly so much as the Horse-shoe one ; the quantity of water passing over it being small in comparison with what goes over the Horse-shoe. When standing on Table Rock, close to the water, I did not feel in the least frightened except by the appearance of its projecting so much over the bottom of the bank. A great quantity of water falls in the middle part of this Fall where

it assumes a very deep green color, but at both sides one sees
nothing but spray as white as snow. It is seldom that a person
can have a distinct view of the water at the bottton of the Falls,
for it is enveloped in fog from the spray which rises in clouds,
a portion of which falls immediately, while the rest is carried
into the atmosphere to join its kindred waters. After viewing
it for some time above I walked down along the side of the
river, for about one quarter of a mile, when I came to the ladder
by which you descend the bank and come to the falling water.
In some writers the descent here is represented as both terrifying
and even attended with some dangor. This is not the case now,
whatever it may have been before. There is an excellent ladder
of twenty-eight steps, fastened at the top to an *arbor vitae*, by
which to descend ; and lately Mr. Forsyth, who keeps the near-
est inn, has erected a covered stairway by which all who choose
may go down on paying one York shilling (6¾ ster.) When
down I walked back towards the Falls. It is rather difficult
walking here on account of the quantity of loose rocks lying
along the water's edge that have fallen from the bank. The
rocks on the bank are remarkably loose and are daily crumbling
away so that I did not feel myself quite secure when walking
below them, as a very small portion of them having fallen upon
me from so great a height would have been a termination to all
my labours. On coming near the Falls you are surprised to be-
hold how greatly the bank is excavated below, so that the top
projects over it a number of yards. This sight is sufficient to
make a person suspicious of standing on Table Rock when he
sees how thin a piece of stone it is that separates him from being
precipitated into the dreadful abyss below. I went close to the
edge of the falling water when, in an instant, I was completely
drenched by the spray. There is a considerable space between
the water and the rock so that a person may go a few feet behind
the Falls, but it is attended with considerable danger. The air
is in violent agitation behind the water and there is nothing but

water and darkness. After all the enquiries that I made I could not learn that any person had ever gone far below the water, and although it has been asserted that some people have passed quite through to the other side, yet I do not believe it ; so confident am I that it is altogether impossible to do this that I would doubt my own sight were I to see it actually performed. Here I saw three snakes almost in the very water, two of the striped and one of what is called the milk kind. I was much surprised to meet with such company in this place. When satisfied with viewing the water I began to examine the vegetable production of this interesting place and found a number of plants which I had not hitherto observed, some of them, however, I had not the pleasure of seeing in blossom. This day was for the most part fair with a few slight showers ; thermometer 82°.

13th. This day I again went to the Falls to satisfy my curiosity and endeavor to discover more plants in their vicinity. When I was on the rocks below the Falls I saw a boat going across the river and being anxious to visit Goat Island I went on it. I had always considered this Island inaccessible to man, but have been informed that some people have been in the habit of visiting it for many years past. They sailed from the American side as far into the stream as the island is situated, at some distance above it, and the waters being shallow they were enabled to reach the island and to return without any danger and with little difficulty. At present, however, there is an excellent bridge from the shore to it by which a waggon may pass over with ease. The water runs here with great impetuosity, and is very rough on account of passing over rocks and shelves, but it is by no means deep. The bridge is supported by large beams of wood fixed together in the form of a parallelogram, and the space in the middle is filled with large stones. There was a former bridge a little higher up than where the present one stands, but it was destroyed by the ice last season. Between the shore and Goat Island, there is another island to which the bridge is carried, and then from this one to Goat Island. The distance from land to the first island is about one hundred aud thirty yards, and from this to Goat Island about ninety yards, so that the whole length of the bridge is two hundred and twenty yards. To cross this bridge every grown person pays twenty-five cents (1½ ster.), children are half price. There is a good road around the island and a considerable portion of the upper end of it is cleared and at present carries a good crop of corn. Its circumference, I suppose, may be at least a mile, and the island contains at present one log house. They cross the river here quite close to the Falls; the river has a considerable swell but is not in any way dangerous. It surprised me to see the water so smooth immediately after falling from so great a height. For a short distance below the Horse-shoe Falls the surface of the water has exactly the appearance of snow when partially frozen, and some of it is carried about in all directions by the wind. Further down it shows violent internal agitation, but is nearly smooth on the surface like the water in the whirlpool below. I imagine that the water's not being much more agitated is caused by the very great depth of the river. The people who ferry here told me that it was above three hundred and forty feet in depth. It is a singular circumstance how this solid rock came to be cut to so great depth, all the surrounding country being level. From viewing the country here a person would readily conclude that the Falls originally were at Queenstown, but the time required for their receding so far by the wearing of the rocks would be a great deal longer than what we believe to be the duration of this earth in its present form. People who live here inform me that in the space of thirty years past the Horse-shoe Fall has assumed its present shape from being nearly straight. Weather to day, fair; thermometer 82.

14th. Cloudy; thermometer 83.

15th. Cloudy, with slight rain; thermometer 80.

16th. Cloudy, with thunder and heavy showers ; thermometer 70. To-day I went to see a burning spring. The water rises in the edge of the St. Lawrence and has a covering over it like a pump. On the top there is a gun-barrel fixed, and on applying fire to its mouth the gas instantly burns with a bluish flame. It appears to be hydrogen gas which is by some means freed from the water and burns on the application of fire.

17th. Cloudy forenoon, clear afternoon; thermometer 78.

18th. This being the last day of my stay in this place I went again to the Falls ; still, after all, I am not satisfied with them, but I think the defect lies in the surrounding country and not in the Falls themselves. I may observe here that when standing on the bank of the river, looking down on the fallen water, when the sun is nearly on one side of you a rainbow is to be seen below, as if on the surface of the water, but at sunrise or sunset you will see one, just as during a shower. The time that I have remained here I have stopped at Lundy's Lane, a place well known by name on account of the bloody battle fought there in the late war. The scene of the battle is scarcely a mile distant from the Falls, on a little eminence, close to the public road. The Americans, although vastly superior in numbers, were driven from the field, a circumstance which they are unwilling to admit. I saw some of the houses here that are literally riddled by the bullets shot during the action. This day was fair ; thermometer 80.

19th. On the 19th, after having packed up and sent to Kingston what specimens I had collected, I departed for Fort Erie. Two miles above the Falls I passed through the village of Chippewa, near which a battle was fought, where 1,500 British were driven from the field by 5,000 of the Americans under General Brown. The Canadian militia suffered severely in this engagement. The road lies alongside the river and the country is thickly settled all along this way. There are a number of islands between the Falls and Lake Erie, the principal of which are Navy Island and Grand Island, the latter being a number of miles in length. The commissioners for settling the boundary between Canada and the United States were encamped on the upper end of Grand Island when I passed it. I came this night to the ferry opposite Black Rock and about a mile below Fort Erie, where I remained for the night. This day was fair; thermometer 82.

20th. Before leaving Canada I went up in the morning to see Fort Erie, which is situated where the St. Lawrence isssues from Lake Erie. I imagined that it was still held by some troops, but on coming to it I found it was a complete ruin. The whole of the buildings and fortifications are destroyed and appear to be as when they were blown up in the war. In my opinion this has been and could be made one of the strongest fortifications in Upper Canada. There is little doubt that if another war should occur between the States and Britain the latter would pay attention to the repairing of the Fort. I breakfasted before I crossed the river. There is a strong current in the river here which makes it difficult to cross. The river is about one-half of a mile in width, and the boats have to set off at least one-quarter of a mile above where they are to land on the opposite side. The charge is a quarter dollar for each person and half a dollar for a horse. You land at Black Rock, which is a scattered village containing between forty and fifty houses. The only house that is anyway conspicuous is that of General Porter; it is a very handsome two-storey building. I did not stop any time here but went on to Buffalo, two miles from this. Buffalo is a large town and contains a number of very elegant buildings. The present town has been all built since the war, it having been burned by the British in retaliation for the burning of Newark (Niagara). I remained a few hours in Buffalo and having gone into a bookseller's shop I was pleased to see an extensive collection of books, and a number of them published in London as late as 1818. When I arrived here I scarcely knew which way I was going next. After examining a map I determined to proceed along the south side of Lake Erie to Erie, or perhaps further, as I should determine when I would reach that place. There is a large creek near Buffalo which must be crossed on going up the lake. This is one inconvenience which a traveller meets with in the States, that if a creek be large he may expect to find no bridge, but should there be one then it has been erected by private individuals who charge toll, so whether in boats or on bridges, you still must pay. I travelled twelve miles from Buffalo and for eight of them along the beach which is as tiresome a road as I have ever travelled on, it being so very soft that one sinks into the sand as if it were snow. This day was fair but cloudy in the afternoon, which made it cooler. I did not see the thermometer to day.

21st. I had an opportunity of riding in a waggon for upwards of twenty miles, and as the road lay close to the lake, and for nearly half the way on the beach, I preferred riding to walking. All along this part of the lake I consider the soil very indifferent, a considerable portion of it being very sandy and some parts of it approaching to clay. For eight miles on this side of Buffalo there is a tract of land belonging to the Indians, a great number of whom reside in this neighborhood and have some villages ; afterwards the houses are pretty frequent along the road. The rye and wheat harvest has begun in a few places. Indian corn appears to grow better here than any other kind of grain, in many places it is very fine. There seems to be a general deficiency in the flax crop in this part of the country ; it is very short owing to the want of sufficient moisture. This country is frequently doomed to suffer severely from want of sufficient rain. I am informed that this season has been very dry and that last season not as much rain fell from the beginning of June until October as would reach the depth of an inch into the ground, which caused a great deficiency in the crops. This road is the worst for wheeled carriages of any that I have ever seen, being so full of stumps and tree roots that it requires great attention to prevent being overturned. Although I had liberty to ride all the way yet in many places I chose to walk rather than suffer the jolting of the wagon. Thirty miles from Buffalo I passed a large creek at a place named Cattaraugus, where there is a tavern and two or three houses. I went on through similar scenery until sunset when I remained for the night at a tavern. This day I found the beautiful *Monarda Kalmiana*, being the first time I had seen this plant. It is very different in appearance from the *Monarda Didyma*, with which it has been confounded. I observed also a species of *Allium* with a bulbous root and a stem about six inches high, but without any leaves, it was not fully blown, but the flower is white. Day fair; thermometer 83. I should have mentioned that in the evening I found a piece of swampy ground covered with the *Rhododendron Maximum*, all in flower. I scarcely ever was more pleased with the sight of a plant than to see this in its native soil.

22nd. I started a little after sunrise and continued my journey. Early in the forenoon I passed through a small village named Fredonia. Since I left Cattaraugus the road has been about a mile and a half distant from the lake; the land is very light. Almost all the wheat is ready for cutting. In a few instances I have observed the people cutting the wheat with sickles but it is generally done with the scythe, and what is called a cradle. Orchards are plentiful here, and more than half of the trees are peach trees which seem to bear large quantities of fruit but I suspect some of them are indifferent in quality none of the trees being grafted. Buckwheat sowing is nearly finished, and in most places the wheat is above ground. As I come through the woods to-day I was surprised to see immense quantities of seedlings of that beautiful tree the *Liriodendron Tulipifera*, without being able to perceive an old one. Although this tree is so distinct from all others, in the singular form of its leaves, yet I afterwards found that I had passed many of them without knowing what they were. I had no conception that this ever grew to such a size and in such a form. The common size of the trunk at the bottom is from three to four feet in diameter and it continues of nearly the same dimensions and remarkably straight to the height of from forty to sixty feet without a single branch or even a leaf. After it begins to branch, the head is but short and looks as if stunted, so that it does not possess the beauty of a young tree. In this part of the country the inhabitants call it the Cucumber tree, from the similarity of its fruit to that of the young cucumber. For nearly the space of two weeks I have enjoyed one very great comfort : no mosquitoes have troubled me. I know now how to appreciate such an exemption. Taverns are generally to be met with along this road every mile or two. I do not think that they can reap much advantage from such an employment, more particularly since the steamboat has run from Black Rock to Detroit, as most of the people going up or down prefer the water to travelling by land. This day was fair with appearance of thunder-showers to the South-east ; in the evening the sky became overcast, and it looked as if it would soon rain ; thermometer 88.

23rd. There was a heavy shower of rain last night, which rendered travelling more agreeable in the morning, but by mid-day you could not perceive that there had been any rain, and the road was remarkably dusty and disagreeable. The morning was cloudy with a considerable breeze. Before noon I had entered the State of Pennsylvania which borders on Lake Erie for a considerable distance. I observed nothing in the country to-day different from what I have seen for some days past. The most of the inhabitants are busily employed in cutting their wheat There is much talk here of war with Britain. I believe that through all the States you will find the Irish to bear the mos inveterate hatred to the British nation and government. This afternoon there was much thunder which went all around here but in the evening there was a considerable shower, which caused me to stop a short time, so that I did not reach Erie this night ; thermometer 92.

24th. This morning I went to Erie, which is about two miles from where I stopped last night. I remained here a little while and took breakfast before I proceeded further. This town is situated upon the shore of the lake. In front of the town there is a large bay, caused by a narrow peninsula, which goes out from the mainland some miles to the westward, and runs down opposite the town, at a distance of from one to two miles. This would be an excellent place for shipping if it were not so shallow. At the mouth of the Bay there is a sand-bank which reaches nearly from the one side to the other, which prevents large vessels from entering it. There is a blockhouse at the extremity of the peninsula, and two war sloops are lying near it. This town is not very extensive yet, but from its situation is likely to increase rapidly, as it is the port for a large tract of country to the southward. The steamboat which sails from Black Rock once every week touches here, and at two or three more places along the lake, and then proceeds to Detroit, where she returns by the same route, She formerly came close to the town, but having one time got aground at the mouth of the bay, she now stops below. This boat made a voyage this spring as far as the Fort of Michilimackinac, on the upper end of Lake Huron, which is the only time that a steamboat has been in that part of the world. I determined now to proceed by the Pittsburgh road instead of going any further up the lake. There is an excellent turnpike from here to Waterford, a town fourteen miles distant. The land appears to be pretty good along this way but it is very thinly settled owing to the proprietors having raised the price to ten dollars per acre while as good can be purchased in the neighbourhood for one dollar. They consider that the turnpike enhances its value so much above that which is situated further back in the country. This day was fair, with some showers ; thermometer 84.

25th. This being Sunday I remained at Waterford all day. In the morning it was fair, but in the afternoon there was a great deal of thunder. A little rain came this way two or three times; thermometer 92.

26th. Having observed some plants yesterday of which I had no specimens, I had alloted this morning before setting out for the purpose of collecting them, but this day proved so rainy that I was obliged to remain here all day without getting anything done. In coming this way from Erie the ground rises greatly for nine miles and for the other five descends considerably so that although Waterford is much lower than the surrounding country, yet I consider it higher than the level of the lake. This town may contain about fifty houses, scarcely any two together, and none of them possessing much external elegance. At a short distance from the town is a small lake called Le Boeuf, which seems to be about one mile in circumference. From this lake runs a small creek by which boats descend to Pittsburgh. The most of travellers, and particularly families of emigrants, purchase boats here and go by water. There are people here who make boats of all kinds and always have a stock on hand ready for travellers. If I had had a botanical companion I would have purchased a skiff and gone by water there being as good a chance of meeting with plants along the edge of the creek as along the road. A boat sufficient to carry two or three people can be purchased for six dollars. Although it did not rain constantly this day yet the woods were so wet that I could do nothing with specimens, so I amused myself with the " Spectator " which at all times is a good and agreeable companion. Thermomeler 73.

27th. This morning being dry, although cloudy and foggy, I collected specimens and about nine o'clock I set out on my journey. After leaving Waterford there is only a very indifferent road, all the making that it has got being only the clearing of trees from it. On account of the late rain it was very muddy.

The greater part of the timber here is oak, and the soil is of a gravelly clay which, however, generally produces good crops. About mid-day I heard the thunder roaring to the westward, which after some time came this way. The rain continued for about two hours during which I remained under cover of an old shed along with some sheep. The sky having again cleared I journeyed southward at a slow pace, the road which was bad before being now a great deal worse. As taverns are scarcer here than in many places in America by the time I reached the first one from Waterford it was near sunset so I remained there for the night. The landlord informed me that "His Excellent Kingship, Joseph Buonaparte," dined here one time in the course of his journey through this state and there being a picture, or rather a caricature, pasted on the wall representing his brother Napoleon on horseback attempting to grasp the Russian Crown, while he was attacked in front by the Russian bear and in the rear by the British lion, Joseph bought this piece and tore it up, displeased to see his brother exhibited in such a disagreeable situation. Thermometer 78.

28th. This morning I crossed the French Creek, which is the same that I mentioned as coming from Lake Le Boeuf. Some places here are thickly settled while others are not so. For a considerable distance the road lies near to the creek and there are some excellent meadow lands in many places on each side of it. In the afternoon I reached the town of Meadville, a considerable village situated in a pleasant locality. It has a printing office and publishes a weekly newspaper. I may here observe that on account of not using stamped paper a weekly paper is sold at the very reasonable rate of two dollars per annum. Immediately after leaving Meadville I had again to cross the creek; at this place there is a covered bridge, an object with which I should always be extremely glad to have nothing to do. I believe it is from early habit that I have acquired so great antipathy to toll bridges. I would feel more satisfied in giving six cents at a ferry than three at a bridge. I only got seven miles from town to-night. The most of the way there are no houses. There are plenty of wild turkeys in this place ; the man with whom I stopped told me that he had shot one to-day. Deer, bear and wolves are not uncommon. I have been enquiring almost every day about rattlesnakes but I find there is no likelihood 'of my meeting with any, a circumstance that gives me much disappointment. They are very uncommon now in this part of the state ; a few may be seen in the course of the season but no considerable number. Almost every person with whom I have discoursed about them pretends to be able to cure their bite. The remedies are all plants of various kinds ; however, I do not place much confidence in their abilities. This day was fair ; thermometer 88.

29th. A great part of this day I travelled through woods, with few houses. The land in general is low-lying and of a swampy nature. I think that by a little labor it could be rendered fit for the purposes of agriculture. The road through the woods is very indifferent on account of too much rain and the little attention paid to keeping it in repair. A turnpike has been commenced between Waterford and Pittsburg, so that when it is finished there will be little travel on this road. I was only able to reach the town of Mercer this evening. This town is in one of the finest situations of any that I have seen in this part of the country, being on a considerable eminence and possessing a larger view of the surrounding country than the most of American towns. The town is but small, with no buildings of notice. There is a printing office here which publishes a weekly paper. This morning there was a fog but the sun soon dispelled it. Day fair ; thermometer 84.

30th. Soon after leaving Mercer I found the country very different from any that I had yet passed through. I now got amongst oaks which were generally only a few feet high so that the country looked as if it had once been cleared and only partially grown again ; however, I believe that it is yet in its natural state. The soil is nothing but gravel and scarcely worth cultivating. To the northward this state is for the most part fairly level, but here it begins to be remarkably uneven. In the course of a day's journey you will not find one mile of the road level, but continually up one hill and down another. These hills, or rather eminences, are of no great height or extent but extremely numerous, and generally of a conical form. There is no art displayed in the plan of the road which is carried straight forward however steep it may be, which renders it extremely severe on horses with loaded waggons. The people here are few in number but what there are of them are generally Irish or of Irish extraction, flaming Republicans. There is a general outcry of " bad times," no money to be seen, banks failing, and all things at a standstill. The banking system is carried to a ruinous extent in this and all the other States. I have seen a list of forty-nine chartered banks in the State of Pennsylvania alone, and for the other States in proportion. Almost every village has or has had a bank, and even private individuals have had banks and passed their bills to a large amount which in a short time are of no value. I have made it a rule at no time to take any of their paper for what you receive in one town very probably will be refused in the next. I did not make much above twenty miles to-day. The weather is beginning to be so hot now that it is extremely fatiguing to walk and carry as heavy a load as I have. To-day fair ; thermometer. 94.

31st. I started at sunrise and set out for Harmony, nine miles distant. For one mile there were some houses, but afterwards it was all woods for eight miles. The woods are much more pleasant to travel through than they generally are, being thin with few bushes of underwood, and the road excellent. I have found this kind of land and these woods to be very productive of a great variety of plants. I saw nothing worthy of notice until I came near Harmony, where I almost thought that I had been transported to some part of the North of Scotland, on account of the appearance of a collection of huts, which had the walls of them been of stone, certainly would have resembled the cottages of the Highlanders. There were a number of them near the road, on both sides, and perhaps in not one out of six might you be able to see any indication of life about them. They were all covered with thatch and certainly were the most ugly, dirty and wretched looking set of houses or hovels that I ever saw, or expect to see in America. Upon inquiry I found that they were built by a colony of Germans twenty-five years ago, but some years since they totally abandoned this part of the country and moved to some other place. About half a mile further I came to the town of Harmony which was built and inhabited by the same colony. Originally it seems to have been built in the same style as described above, but at present there are about a dozen brick houses in the town, but all extremely inelegant, having high steep roofs. On a little hill near the town there has been expended a great deal of labour to cut it in on one side in the form of stairs, and on these vines were planted. However, since the Germans left the place the vines have been destroyed by cattle. I think it probable that vines would do well here. A small muddy creek passes this place over which there was a bridge but it had fallen lately, so that you have to pass over on a kind of raft of old boards awkwardly put together. I went eleven miles beyond this to-night when I was stopped by rain. This day was extremely hot ; I never before perspired so much in one day as I did in this. All my clothes were as if they had been in a river. After breafast I eat no more to-day, but drank so much that in the evening I felt rather sick. About 5 p.m. there was a good deal of thunder and a small shower, and after sunset there was a very severe thunder storm which continued some hours. The thermometer for the greater part of the day stood above 90 ; the highest that I observed was 96.

August 1st.   This day being Sunday I stopped here all day, and indeed I had little inclination for travelling or exertion of any kind.   The forenoon was fair; in the afternoon there was a thunder storm : thermometer 88.

2nd.   After breakfast I set out for Pittsburgh, which is fourteen miles from here, and arrived there in the afternoon. The country here is the most uneven of any that I ever saw, and yet there are no hills of any consequence.   The soil is very barren in many places.   The oats may be worth cutting with the scythe but not with the hook.   It is the general practice here to finish the wheat and rye harvest before cutting the hay, so that the latter in many places is not yet cut.   I did not obtain a view of Pittsburgh until I was very near it on account of its low-lying situation.   Before entering the town you have to cross the Alleghany River which is about four hundred yards wide.   There is a very fine bridge being built across the river here, consisting of five very large arches supported by stone piers, the upper part being of wood.   Pittsburgh is situated on an angle formed by the junction of the Alleghany and Monongahela rivers which afterwards assume the name of Ohio.   The town is large and has a number of good brick houses in it, but it has a black and gloomy aspect, on account of the great number of furnaces about the place which burn only pit coal.   There is a vast quantity of coal all around this region which can be mined at very little cost, and this causes it to be used in preference to wood.   On the south side of the Monongahela there is a ridge of hills three hundred feet high, which rise very abruptly from the river and can be ascended in only a few places : they are named the Coal Hills.   This town is the capital of this western country, from which the West are supplied with manufactures. Almost all the emigrants of the West pass through here and descend the Ohio in boats.   In the summer season there is not much water trade here on account of the lowness of the river. At present I saw only a few small boats lying here and a steamboat on the stocks.   The first places that I always visit when in a town are the booksellers shops.   Here I found an excellent and extensive collection of books on almost all the sciences and even some on Botany, a subject on which I scarcely expected to find any.   They have the London and Edinburgh Reviews and all the late popular publications in Britain.   As soon as they come to America they are reprinted in a less expensive form so that you can purchase books for almost one-third of their London price.   The town contains ten or eleven thousand inhabitants, natives of all nations.   In former times when the French possessed Canada they had a fort here at the confluence of the two rivers, which was named Fort du Queene and served as a connecting post between their northern and southern colonies. General Braddock was sent to take it by the British in 1755, but by his foolish bravery and want of caution he was surprised by the French and Indians near here and lost the most of his army, and he himself was mortally wounded.   The field where he was shot is nine miles from Pittsburgh and is still esteemed on account of its being one of the first scenes where General Washington distinguished himself.   This town, or rather where the town is, was for some time called Fort Pitt, from which it has obtained its present name.   This day was fair and hot ; thermometer 94.

3rd.   I now consider that I ought to commence my return journey, it being necessary for me to be in Montreal by the middle of September.   I remained in town till near noon, when I crossed the Alleghany and returned by the road by which I came to town.   My present determination is to go by Franklin, then along the Alleghany till I reach York State, whence I will proceed to Sackett's Harbour where I can get a steamboat for Kingston.   This morning was very foggy : it afterwards cleared and was very hot.   About 2 p.m. I was stopped by a very heavy thunder storm which continued for about four hours with little intermission.   I came to where I had remained on Sunday, at which place the Franklin road leaves the one to Harmony, etc. Thermometer 94.

4tb. This morning was dull and foggy. I packed all my articles and prepared to move homewards. I did not get away until after noon, and travelled twelve miles. This road is not so public as the one on which I had been formerly travelling. The houses are very few in number and the land very sterile. This is a very poor country to all appearances, one good point about it however is that it is a healthy country, chiefly owing to its want of stagnant waters. This seems to be the peculiar land of thunder. This afternoon there was much thunder to the east, but it went round at some distance from this. Thermometer 86.

5th. I again got into the woods, finding occasionally a house after some miles walking. The road is tolerably good for foot travellers but does not seem to be much trodden. I am informed that early in the summer a number of people pass up this way after having been down at Pittsburgh with rafts. I make it my business at every house to inquires about rattlesnakes, but I never can see any, although they are occasionally killed all along the way during summer and both people and cattle are sometimes bitten by them; few however of either die. The inhabitants all have infallible cures, and all different ones. In the evening I reached a very respectable tavern where I remained this night. About sunset it began to lighten and the sky continued for a considerable time in a blaze without the least intermission. The storm came this way, but the rain was not so heavy as might have been expected from the thunder and lightening. This day was fair; thermometer 88.

6th. When I awoke this morning it was still thundering, so that it was rather late before I set off through the bush. During the forenoon there were a few houses to be seen at some distance from one another. This is still a poor barren looking country scarcely able to support any inhabitants. In the afternoon I travelled through an uninhabited wood for about eight miles.

Formerly some people had lived here, as I saw a few houses now in a state of dilapidation and some orchards along the road. The woods here are generally of oak, very thin and the trees not large, with abundance of suckers and herbaceous plants, so that you have the extent of your horizon considerably larger than it commonly is. I think that fire at some period, not very distant, has overrun the woods here which causes them to be so open and destitute of trees. Having gone along some miles I began to descend considerably. At this place I passed great masses of sandstone detached from the rocks. The country here is one continuous rock which is all sandstone. In decending this declivity I passed a spot of remarkably red earth, where a little boy and girl were spreading it as if to dry, and which, upon inquiry, they said was for making paint with. In a short time I reached Sandy Creek, at which place there is a tavern. The common drink all through this part of the country is whiskey, a liquor which is very different however from Scotch whiskey. I was now four and one half miles distant from the town of Franklin where I wished to be to-night, so I marched on and arrived just in time to escape a heavy thunder storm which had commenced some hours ago to the westward. The lightening was terrific, being mostly of that destructive kind called zig-zag, which is a most appropriate name for it. Day fair; thermometer 86.

7th. Franklin is a town containing a few houses scattered over a piece of flat meadow-land, at the junction of French Creek with the Alleghany. It will never be a place of much importance from the nature of the surrounding country. I now expected to get completely into a wilderness for more than one hundred miles. Having crossed French Creek I commenced my peregrinations. For the space of two miles I found some houses but afterwards I travelled seven or eight miles before I saw another. The road here is nothing but a footpath through the woods and in some places scarcely perceptible. The ground is very rocky and the woods are of the same kind as those I travelled through yesterday. It is very uncomfortable walking on this footpath which is hollowed out leaving stones and tree roots projecting on either side, which at almost every step one strikes with his feet ; a circumstance which happened to me very often, as I had to look so much around me that I had little leisure to attend to my feet. Having at length arrived at a house I found that I was at Oil Creek, so named from the oil which rises on its surface in many places. It is thick and of a dark brown color, having a strong disagreeable smell. It rises so copiously that a barrel of it may be collected in a short time. Some soldiers marching to Detroit were the first discoverers of this substance here. The weather had been wet, and from being much exposed to its influences most of the men had been seized with rheumatism, particularly in their joints. In the course of their journey they happened to encamp beside this creek and seeing the oil they determined to try its effects in their disorder. Having rubbed the parts affected sufficiently with it the cure was performed in a short time. Since that time the oil has been collected and sold in many parts of the States. I again went into the woods and found a house three miles from this. The next house I came to was nine miles distant, from which it was three more to a tavern, which I arrived at just before another thunder storm had reached there. The storm was a pretty severe one. I am now so accustomed to the storms that I expect one every evening, however fair the day may prove to be. This morning was very foggy ; afterwards the day was fair and very hot. The heat was very severe upon me having so heavy a load upon my back and a book in each hand, which encumbered me so much that I had difficulty in keeping my eyes and mouth clear of perspiration. Thermometer 90.

8th. To-day I had intended to have looked over and dried all my specimens, and after that to go ten miles which was the distance to the next tavern. Having taken breakfast, and the sky being so cloudy that I could not dry my specimens, I went on, expecting that the afternoon would be more clear. After a few miles I came into low moist pine woods, which continued until I came to the Alleghany about eight miles from where I started. The river here is of considerable size with a number of small islands scattered in it. The land is very high on each side, there being a house only where there is any alluvial soil. When I was standing at the side of the river here I saw three deer swim across to an island. They were not more than three hundred yards distant from me and did not show the slightest timidity, although I was so near them. I had not gone far when it began to rain a little. When I came to the tavern I saw that it was useless to think of drying specimens, so I proceeded to the next tavern five miles from this one, but before I reached it I was completely wet. I had some difficulty in preventing my plants from receiving any injury. The road was now remarkably muddy and fatiguing, so I abode here for the night. Day, generally cloudy ; thermometer 76.

9th. This morning looked still cloudy and looking as if it would rain. I set off for Warren. The road lies close alongside the river the next part of the way. For the first six miles there are few houses, but for six miles on this side of Warren the river side is fairly well settled. I arrived at the town of Warren in the afternoon, but could not go further to-day, as the next house along my road is fourteen miles distant. This town is a county town, although I do not think there are twenty houses in it. Its situation upon the Alleghany is pleasant. The few people that live here seem to frequent the tavern oftener than is consistent with proper economy and industry. Being soon to leave the State of Pennsylvania, I may say a few things about the treatment that I have met with while in it. I have found the most of the inhabitants where I have been, to be Irish who are in general civil people, but bear a great hatred to the British Government. Travelling in this place is much more reasonable than in Canada. The common charges are for a meal of vituals 2/ and 2/26 York, for bed /6, and their spirituous drink is whiskey, which is /6 per gill. The taverns in the States are very different from any idea that could be formed of them from having seen only the Scotch inns. In a tavern here there are not seperate rooms for different persons, but all remain in what they call their bar-room, one corner of which is elevated and contains the liquors. There is no distinction nor difference among people in a tavern, not even between the President and the poorest person. You can have liquors by the glass or half gill all over America, which is by far the best way. Many times in Scotland I have found it extremely difficult to procure lodgings even where there were plenty of taverns, but such is not the case in this country. When you can find a tavern you find lodgings if you wish. When a person comes to a tavern here he never asks if he can have lodging, but takes that for a thing about which there is no doubt. I have found the beds generally very good and all feather ones. In upper Canada they are exceedingly infested with bugs, but here the bugs are not nearly so numerous. Last night I slept none on account of fleas, insects which I have not before met with this summer. In this, along with many other places in both the States and Canada, the inhabitants are subjected to some great inconveniences. There are three things in particular which would operate strongly against my settling in this country. They are the long distance from a church and school, and from a surgeon, besides the fact that a person has a very confined circle of people with whom he can associate. These wants I consider as a balance to many inconveniences that must be endured in many other places. This day when walking along the river side I passed a few Indians who were busily employed in partly roasting and partly smoking venison. They had the deer cut into small pieces and a number of them stuck upon a rod which was then placed near a fire. This day fair ; thermometer 80.

10th. Being now about to commence to go a sixty mile journey through a forest I did not enter the woods until I had taken some breakfast. When I was about to set off, luckily there came a man who was taking the same route, thus I had company all the way. After leaving Warren we crossed the Conewango Creek and travelled by a foot path through the woods for fourteen miles when we reached a house where a tavern was kept. The rest of the woods were of the open sort and the ground very high and rocky, unfit ever to be cultivated. When we arrived at the tavern we concluded to remain here this night, it being fourteen miles to the next white man's house. This morning was very foggy; day fair; thermometer 87.

11th. Our party having now amounted to three we started before sunrise and took the woods. This day we travelled pretty near the river. We passed many Indian houses but the people did not appear to be numerous. I believe that a number were out hunting. In some places they have respectable houses and farms. After travelling twelve miles we went into an Indian's and by words and signs made the squaw give us bread and milk for breakfast. She did not understand much English and could speak none. Continuing our journey we went through a village having a church and school for the Indians. About 4 p.m. we reached a farm house thirty miles from where we started in the morning and remained there this night. It was with difficulty that we could procure any supper and when we got it there was not a sufficiency to satisfy our appetites. Day fair; thermometer 88.

12th. We arose at daybreak and continued our journey. The road was much the same as that travelled on yesterday, and for the greater part of the way to Olean very muddy. Having travelled fourteen miles we came to a house newly built in the woods, where we had breakfast, after which we proceeded to Olean Point, or Hamilton, a small village situated on the Alleghany where navigation begins. Most of the people who are going down the Ohio proceed from here by water. This town has a printing office and publishes a newspaper. This is the most extortionate place that I have been in in the States. The land is very worthless and is not much cultivated. After stopping a short time here I took the road for Geneva. This is a public road although it is very indifferent. I came within seven miles of Olean to-night. The houses are pretty thick along the road but they are much of the same style as those that I have seen since I left Waterford, being miserable looking log huts. I left Warren I expected to find many rare plants along the Alleghany, but found not one that I had not formerly seen. At Olean my two companions left me as they travelled faster than I was able or even wished to do. I generally prefer to travel alone when I have no one with me that is interested in the same pursuits that I am. This day was fair; thermometer 90.

13th. There having been rain last night the road this morning was very muddy and disagreeable. However in a short time it became better. For the space of five miles after I started I passed through a wood, without any houses but all the day afterwards there were plenty of them along the road. The land is all stones or gravel and very uneven, so that there is but a small proportion of it that can be cultivated. The predominating wood is pine, with a few of the harder woods interspersed. This night I reached the village of Angelica, thirty-two miles from Olean. It is like the most of the American villages but small and incompact. This day was fair; thermometer 86.

14th. There is a turnpike from Angelica to Bath, a distance of forty miles. It is generally pretty good but very steep in many places, owing to the great inequality of the ground, and its being carried forward without any regard to the formation of the country. For a considerable distance this morning I passed very few houses, but towards noon they became more plentiful. Along this road there is still much wheat to cut, and although this was an excellent day for that purpose yet no person was to be seen in the fields. I was informed that the greater part of the inhabitants in this place was of a sect which they call sabbatarians. I am ignorant of how far their tenets and general principles agree with those of the Jews, but in the observation of Saturday as their Sabbath they are both alike. This being Saturday there was no outdoor work done. In the afternoon I came to a small village or rather the rudiments of one, called Canister, where I remained for the night. I only travelled twenty miles to-day but it was remarkably fatiguing on account of the great heat. This morning was foggy and there were heavy thunder-looking clouds to be seen at intervals throughout the day; thermometer 88.

15th. This day, whether it should be good or bad, I had alloted for rest. However, it proved a very wet morning, so that at any rate I would have been obliged to stop. Last night I met the surgeon of this place and I spent this day at his house where I was very kindly entertained both by him and his wife. This day continued cloudy with some heavy showers; thermometer 78.

16th. There was a great deal of rain last night and this morning, but after sunrise it appeared to be clearing. Having had breakfast I commenced my journey. The road to-day was remarkably uneven, so that if it was more difficult to walk on it was also more clean, the road being almost dry as soon as it ceased to rain. This is an excellent country in which to make roads, as they require no stones or gravel put on them, but only need to be cut into a proper form. About noon there was a very heavy shower accompanied with some thunder. I was not far distant from a house when it commenced but before I could reach it I was completely wet. After it faired I went on but had not gone far when I had to stop a second time. During the afternoon it appeared alternately to fair and to rain, with occasional thunder. I was again overtaken by a shower and was as wet as before. I was determined that I would not pass a tavern, and I had scarcely reached one when it began to rain and continued raining a considerable part of the night. About one-half of the house in which I lodged allowed the rain to pass through it very copiously, so that although I got a good fire, I had difficulty in keeping myself from being wetter than when I came in. I had determined to reach Bath to-night, but was stopped three and one-half miles from it. Although the road here is a turnpike yet it is as much overgrown with grass and weeds as if it were a meadow, and in many places it is fit for mowing, which indicates that travellers are not numerous here. This morning was very hot; the thermometer about 8 a.m. was 84, but in the afternoon it was cooler.

17th. I was delayed by rain from setting out before seven this morning. I travelled to Bath where I breakfasted. This is a considerable sized village containing some neat wooden houses. There is a man here who is about to commence great manufactories of cloth and oil. I read an advertisement of his in the papers, in which he invites the people to assist him and endeavour to expel the British manufactories from their country. This town has a weekly newspaper which seems to be in favour of Governor Clinton's administration. There is another here about to commence, which is to be anti-Clintonian. After leaving Bath I passed through rocky ground covered with small shrubby oaks. At six miles distant I came to a lake of about twenty miles in length, and apparently of one in breadth, named Crooked Lake. At a little distance from it on both sides the country is more thickly settled than any that I have seen for a long time past. In the afternoon I passed the north end of a small body of water which is named Little Lake, and is thickly settled all around. I made twenty miles from Bath and rested for the night. This night a man lately come from Albany lodged here, who informed me that there are great apprehensions of a war with Spain, on account of her not ratifying the treaty for the cession of the Floridas to the United States. Great Britain is generally considered to be the instigator of Spain to resist the demands of America. The yellow fever is said to be very prevalent in New York at this time. This day has been cloudy, inclining oftentimes to fog ; thermometer 76.

18th. This morning was extremely foggy, so that I was involved in darkness for some time after commencing my journey. The road and country continued much the same as for some distance westward. By noon I reached the lower end of Crooked Lake where there are a number of mills and a considerable sized village, named Penn Yan. I observed nothing about it worthy of particular notice. A newspaper is published here. I proceeded through a thickly inhabited country, the crops everywhere promising great abundance of the necessaries of life. About sunset I got in sight of Seneca Lake and the town of Geneva, where I halted for the night, having travelled to-day twenty-six miles. This day was fair ; thermometer 81.

19th. Geneva is situated at the north end of Lake Seneca. The ground rises considerably from the water's edge which makes an agreeable outlook from the town. This is by far the handsomest town that I have yet met with in the States and is pretty large. A great number of the houses are built of wood, which have a very neat and elegant appearance when properly painted. Seneca Lake is between 38 and 40 miles in length, but its breadth is only a few miles. The soil around this is greatly superior to any that I have seen for some time and is well improved. Last evening I overtook a man travelling in my direction so we agreed to keep one another company, This morning we started before sunrise and continued our journey eastward. The road here is a turnpike and is very good. Having gone seven miles we came to the village of Waterloo, which although not compactly built contains some of the best houses that I have seen in America. A number of them are of brick. About three miles further we passed the village of Seneca Falls. Thirteen miles from Geneva we came to Cayuga Lake across which there is a wooden bridge a little more than a mile long. This lake is nearly the same size and shape as Lake Seneca. Six cents are charged for each foot passenger crossing here. In the afternoon we came to Auburn a large and handsome village which will be rendered important on account of the new State prison in course of erection here. It was considered necessary to have another one in addition to the one already in the city of New York. There is a great part of this building finished and as much to do as will take three years to finish. At present there are about 200 prisoners in it and it is to have apartments for two thousand. If the laws are not made more severe I believe that this State will soon require more prisons. Crimes seem to be very frequent here. This town possesses many fine brick buildings and I consider the Presbyterian Church, which is of wood, the handsomest building of its kind that I have seen. The land from Geneva to Auburn is more of a sandy than a gravelly nature and it seems superior in quality to any that I have seen in this State. Crops everywhere are abundant, but there is a general outcry about the scarcity of cash. All the trading that is carried on is wholly by barter. A person here having a little silver or gold could find great bargains. Wheat can be bought at half a dollar a bushel for ready money, and other things in proportion. I saw a man who had great difficulty in selling excellent lamb at five cents per pound. To-day we travelled about twenty-seven miles The sky was cloudless and it was exceedingly hot; thermometer 91.

20th. This morning we set out very early in order to take it easier during the heat of the day. We were now approaching the celebrated salt springs of Onondaga, where more salt is made than at any other place in America. A few miles from the springs the ground becomes covered with small oaks, and has a sterile appearance. In the afternoon we reached the salt-works which are four miles distant from the village of Onondaga. Here I was again left to myself having determined to remain a day or two at this place. This day was fair and hot. The heat has been increasing very much for a few days; thermometer 92.

21st. As I remain here to-day, I may give a few sketches of this place; There is a small village here named Salina which is only a short distance to the south of Lake Onondaga. The land around the village is very low and swampy. Between the buildings and the lake is a flat piece of ground partially covered with water which is all salt and which is called the springs. I could not observe the water rise in any particular spot, but for the space of two or three acres it looked like a spot that had been covered with water during winter but now nearly dry and covered with all manner of rubbish and filth, sending forth a most diagreeable odour. The furnaces for drying the salt are in and around this spot. There is communication by water between this and Ontario by which salt is carried to Canada and the Western States. I have never been in a more disagreeable and unhealthy place than this. At this time a number of people were sick with fever and ague, a disease which is always to be found here. It it were not for the salt works I believe this never would be a village. Salt forms the only circulating medium about this part of the country, instead of money of which there is scarcely any. When a person brings anything to be sold the first question is, " how much salt will he take ?" Every day numbers of waggons arrive from different parts of the country to purchase salt in exchange for flour, butcher's meat, etc. The price of salt is remarkably low, being only 1/York per bushel. A barrel of salt, containing five bushels, can at this time be purchased for 5/York (2/9¾ ster.) and as much for the duty. The most of the States are supplied with salt from this place. Within a mile of Salina there pass three branches of the Great Western Canal which is to join the waters of Lake Erie to the Hudson River near Albany. The distance is about three hundred miles. None of the canal here is nearly finished, and from its great length and the nature of the country through which it is to pass, it is an arduous undertaking and will require the labour of years. This day was fair and hot ; thermometer 92.

22nd. This morning was cloudy and there fell a few drops of rain. I did not wish to travel to-day, but before noon I found that I could enjoy no satisfaction in the house where I lodged on account of the number of idlers who frequented it. It must give uneasiness to any person who has any regard for religion to witness the general inattention to even the external duties of the Sabbath, both in the States and in Canada. Instead of preserving a tolerably decent behaviour on that day, it is commonly spent in drinking, shooting, fishing, or some such amusement, and that even by many who consider themselves to have good moral characters. Any person newly arrived in this country could not recognize a Sabbath at all. No doubt there are many people who behave otherwise, but they certainly are in the minority. Being completely disgusted with this place I cleared out (to use a Yankee phrase) and went on seven miles when I stopped at a tavern that was not so well supplied with people. Before I reached it there was some rain, and it showered occasionally during the afternoon. Thermometer 80.

23rd. There was a remarkable alteration in the weather this morning. Instead of a suffocating heat it was disagreeably cool. I set out on the way to Sackett's Harbour. This road, I believe, was chiefly made during the war to facilitate the transportation of military and naval stores to the harbour. For many miles it goes through swampy woods, and is formed of logs placed longitudinally across the road. This is the universal practice in this country in forming or mending the road in moist land. Twelve miles from Salina I crossed by a ferry the Oneida river at a little distance to the west from where it issues from the lake of the same name. Very great quantities of eels are caught in this lake and river. The greater part of the day I was surrounded by woods, the houses being few in number. The land here does not seem to be worth much. I have seen farms to-day that I would not take in a present, they are so barren. Crops are greatly deficient here from want of rain; the ground is as if it had been burnt. Potatoes will be very scarce this winter; they are expected to be near a dollar per bushel. This day was so cold that even when travelling I could not keep myself comfortable. It was rather cloudy with a high wind; thermometer 70.

24th. This morning was clear, calm, and very cold. A sunrise the thermometer was 45. I pursued my journey and having gone seven miles I came to Salmon River where there are a number of houses. As I came from this I met a great number of waggons loaded with men and women going to a Methodist camp-meeting near Salmon river. These meetings are common in this country and are held for a number of days, generally in the woods. As the man with whom I travelled for two days from Geneva, lived near my road, I intended to stop a night at his house which I reached in the afternoon. Having been pretty well treated I went to bed, but as it happened I did not enjoy much repose. Some time about midnight there came a number of men with lights, who ordered us all to clear out or they were going to pull down the house; and they were as good as their word, for they actually did so. They took out all the furniture and in a short time there was not one log left upon another. The demolishers were the neighbours, and for certain reasons which I did not exactly know they were determined to have this family out of the neighbourhood, and this was the method adopted to effect it. Thus I was obliged to take my knapsack and march. I was not so fortunate as to find a shed where I could remain till the morning. I lay down by the road side for a short time, but I soon became very cold and wet with dew, so I took the road once more and soon came to a place where trees were burning, where I remained and smoked my pipe until daybreak, and then went on for Sackett's Harbour. This day was fair; thermometer 76.

Aspidum Goldianum.

Mr. Goldie's Original Description.

Sori subrotundi sparsi. *Indusium* umbilicatum vel uno latere dehiscens.

Aspidium *Goldianum*; frondibus ovato-oblongis glabris pinnatis, pinnis lanceolato-acuminatis pinnatifidis, laciniis oblongis spinuloso-serratis, stipite paleaceo.

Hab. Near Montreal.

From one and a half to two feet in height. Allied to *Aspidium Cristatum* more than to any other species in the genus; but abundantly distinguishable by the greater breadth of the frond, which gives quite a different outline, and by the form of the pinnae, which are never *broader* at the base, but are, on the contrary *narrower* than several of the segments just above them. These segments, too, are longer and narrower, slightly falcate, and those of the lowermost pinnae are never lobed, but simply serrated at the margin. The serratures are likewise terminated by more decided, though short, spinules. The *fructifications* are central near the midrib, and this circumstance prevents the species from bearing, as it would otherwise do, no inconsiderable affinity to *A. marginale*.

Specimens of this plant, cultivated in the Botanic Garden at Glasgow, from roots which I brought from Canada, retain all the characters which I have above described.

CPSIA information can be obtained
at www.ICGtesting.com
Printed in the USA
LVOW13s1554050217
523250LV00005B/388/P